# TEXTILES

© *Rupa Classic India Series 1993*
*First published 1993 by Rupa & Co.*
*7/16 Ansari Road, Daryaganj, New Delhi-110 002*
*Second impression 1998*
*Set in 9.6 on 12 Palatino by Fototype, New Delhi*
*Printed in India by R.N. Polyplast Pvt. Ltd., Noida*

*ISBN 81-7167-211-6*

*Design: KD Prashad*
*General Editor: Amrita Kumar*

# TEXTILES

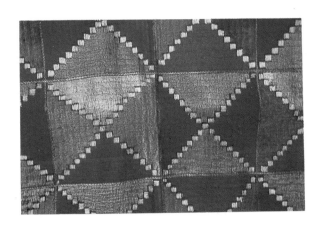

*Photographs by Ashish Khokar*

Rupa & Co

# INTRODUCTION

*Sage Markanda, it is said, was the weaver of the gods, who fashioned the first fabric from lotus fibre. Even today, the weavers of Kancheepuram in Tamil Nadu claim descent from him.*

*The history of Indian textiles is as old as the gods, as colourful as the civilization from which it emerged. A complex social structure, a cultural and religious life strewn with rituals, ceremonies and festivals dictated an elaborate textile vocabulary. Religious traditions also demanded the finest fabric to clothe the deities. Under the patronage of kings and queens, these traditions evolved further to produce grander, more elaborate textiles.*

*Under the Mughals, Indian weavers worked alongside masters from Persia and Central Asia, assimilating new skills in weaving and ornamentation. The Naqshbandi art of tying designs into looms emerged from this cultural contact as did the floral designs of Kashmir.*

*Reeling under competition from machine-made imitations, Indian textiles declined in the nineteenth and twentieth centuries. In the mid-twentieth century, Mahatma Gandhi converted the dying art of spinning into a symbol of self-reliance and freedom. It was a new lease of life. Today the grand textiles traditions live on, inspired by a rich history and fuelled by the artistic stamina of the Indian craftsman.*

*Woman from the Tunda village in Kutch.*
*The* odhni *(head-cover) is patterned by the*
bandhni *or tie-and-dye technique.*

Cover: Phulkari *bedspread, Punjab.*

Above and right: *Single*-ikat *saris, Andhra Pradesh.*

Overleaf: Patola *or double*-ikat *sari, Gujarat.*

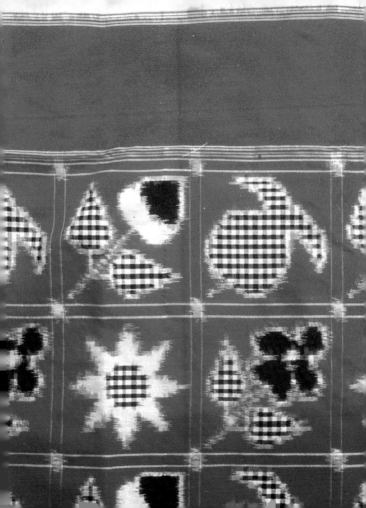

*Single*-ikat *sari, Orissa.*

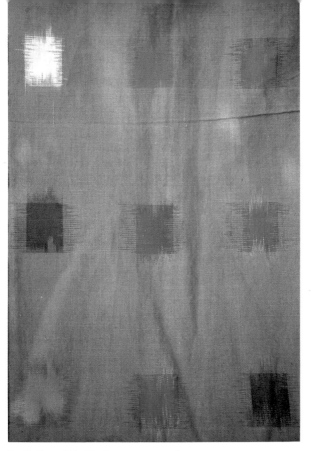

*Imitation of the* ikat *weave on contemporary furnishing fabric.*

*How many know*
*the world-weaver*
*who spread the warp?*

*Earth and Sky,*
*the two beams of his loom.*

*Sun and Moon,*
*Two shuttles filled and ready.*

*He takes a thousand threads.*
*He spreads them lengthwise.*
*Watch him as he weaves today.*

*The* cir: *the length end*
*is still far away,*
*most difficult to reach.*

*Says Kabir: Karma with Karma*
*woven with unwoven threads.*
*How well*
*this weaver weaves.*

This *bhajan* (devotional song) and the one on page 23
were composed by Kabir, 15th century, Benaras. Kabir
was a mystic-poet, a non-conformist social thinker, a
weaver, an integrator. Many of his songs carry
metaphors of the weaver and his craft.

Jamdani *sari, Andhra Pradesh.*

Jamdani *sari, Andhra Pradesh.*

16

# TYPES OF LOOMS

**Loin loom:** *To operate this, the weaver sits on the ground, legs outstretched. The yarn is attached to a belt around the weaver's waist at one end and at the other, to a fixture in the house. The loom is operated by hand, with the weft threaded through with the aid of a bamboo stick.*

**Pit loom:** *The loom is placed inside a pit with the warp threads stretched outside it. The weaver sits at the edge of the pit to operate the pedals.*

**Throw-shuttle loom:** *Here the bobbin is passed through the warp by hand.*

**Fly-shuttle loom:** *The output of this loom is much higher than that of the throw-shuttle loom. The shuttle is thrown from side to side while beating is done by pulling the stay by hand.*

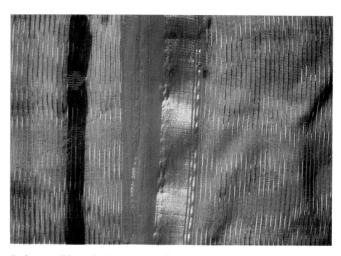

Laheria Chanderi *sari, Madhya Pradesh.*

Kota *sari, Rajasthan.*

Kancheepuram *sari, Tamil Nadu.*

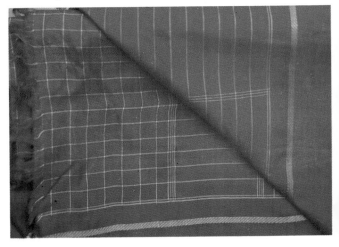

Paithani *sari, Maharashtra.*

*Fine, finely woven is this spread*
*Tell of which warp, and tell what fills,*
*Of which thread woven, is this spread?*
*With nervé threads of the sun and moon,*
*With Pure-Thread that seeks its end.*
*Eight maidens spin and this wheel swings*
*With the five elements the warp is laid*
*Ten months to ready it, the Maker takes.*
*Close, closely woven is this spread.*
*This, men, the gods and sages wear.*
*And in the wearing, some they soil*
*Kabir, Truth-Server, wore from birth*
*This spread; now homing, leaves it as it is;*
*Fine, finely woven is this spread.*

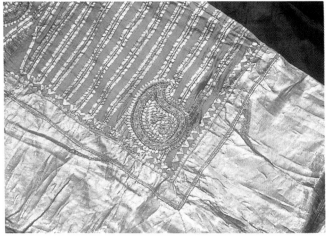

Zari *work on royal* odhni, *Jaipur.*

Right: *Brocaded royal sari, Benaras.*

Overleaf: Kinari *work on royal* ghagra *(skirt), Jaipur.*

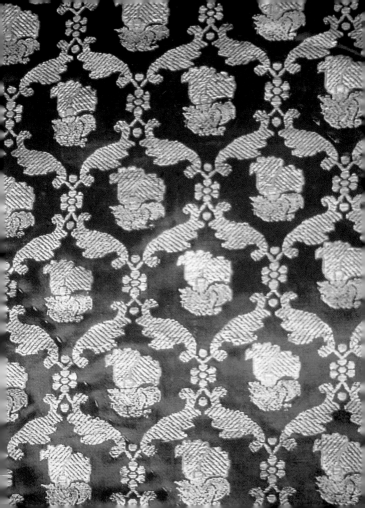

*Royal throne, Jodhpur.*

*Brocade attire at Rajput wedding.*

*Detail of royal carpet, Benaras, 19th century.*

*Zardozi with stone inlay on velvet royal tunic, Jaipur*

Chikan *embroidery, Lucknow.*

Kantha *embroidery, West Bengal.*

*Tribal motif, Bastar.*

*Tribal motif, Kutch.*

*Embroidery on indigo, Ahmedabad.*

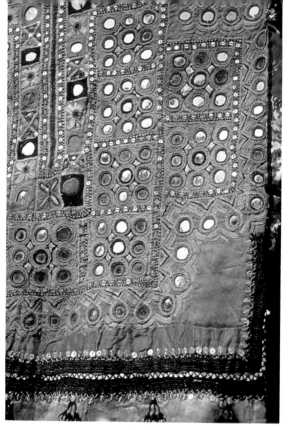

*Mirror work, Kutch.*

**Overleaf:** *Detail of antique Moghul dress.*

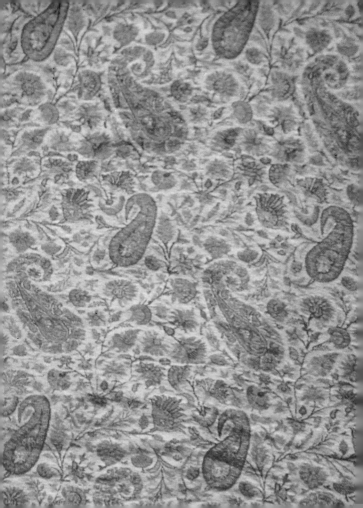

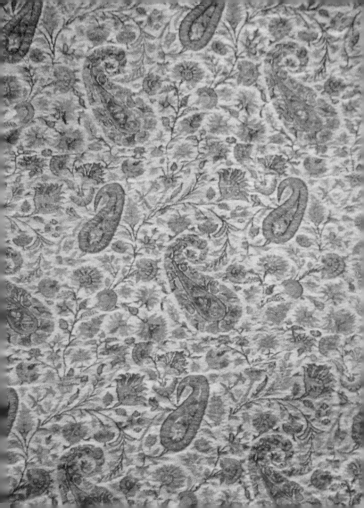

*Applique quilt cover, Saurashtra.*

*Embroidered bag with cowrie shells, Saurashtra.*

*Detail of embroidered royal* ghagra, *Jamnagar.*

*Detail of embroidered royal* ghagra, *Jamnagar.*

*Barmer nomads in printed* odhnis.

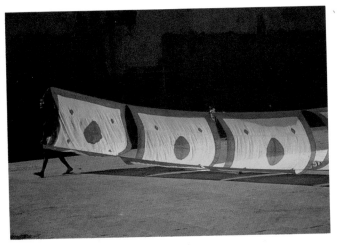

Bandhni odhnis, *Rajasthan.*

Bandhni *turban, Rajasthan.*

# THE SIGNIFICANCE OF COLOUR

**Red** *is for lovers, its different shades reflecting the states of love. Manjitha or madder is the strongest as it can never be washed away. Crimson is worn by brides as it signifies eternal marital bliss. Red is also the colour of Brahma and of the festival, Dussehra.*

**Yellow** *is the colour of northern wheat, of mustard harvests, of Spring, of mango blossoms, of the cry of mating birds, of fertility. It is also the colour of the festival, Holi.*

**Saffron** *or gerua signifies martyrdom. It is for yogis, for wandering minstrels, seers, poets who renounce the earth.*

**Blue** *is the colour of Krishna and of Vishnu. It reflects the fury of the eastern monsoon, of rain clouds. Another shade of blue, hari nila, is the reflection of the sky in water. Blue is worn by a woman going to meet her lover at night.*

**White** *is for purity. It is also the colour of Shiva. Ancient Indian texts speak of the many tones of white: ivory, jasmine, cream, pearl, mist, the August moon, August clouds after the monsoon, the conch shell.*

*Hand block-printed sari, Sanganer.*

*Hand block-printed motif, Sanganer.*

*Gold-embossed* ghagra, *Kutch.*

*Right: Detail of heat-embossed antique Moghul*
angarkha *(male dress).*

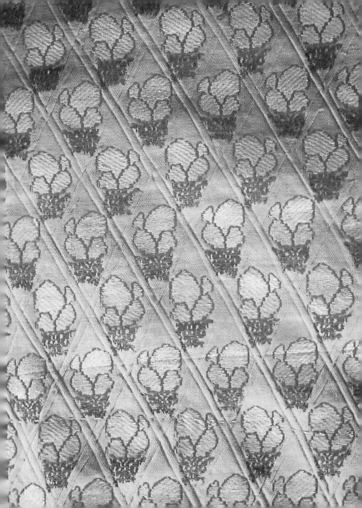

# THE WHEEL OF FREEDOM

*Hand-spun and woven fabrics were for centuries an integral part of India's rich textile tradition. Under colonial rule, which coincided with the Industrial Revolution in Europe, India was reduced to becoming a supplier of cotton to the textile mills of Manchester, Birmingham and Lancashire. The handloom weaver was virtually wiped out from the market as the country was forced to accept cloth of inferior quality manufactured in England.*

*During the freedom struggle, Indian nationalists, spurred by Mahatma Gandhi's missionary zeal, started the boycott of foreign goods as part of the Swadeshi Movement. Cloth from England was burned publicly and Indians started wearing hand-spun* khadi *in defiance of the Empire's economic exploitation of India. Once more the whirr of the* chakra *(spinning wheel) sounded across the length and breadth of the country. In converting the act of spinning and weaving into a political weapon, a dying village industry had been revived.*

*As one of the factors that brought a mighty colonial empire to its knees, the* chakra *become a symbol of freedom. When India finally achieved independence, it was given a place of honour at the centre of the Indian flag.*

*Woollen weave, Kulu.*

Shahtoosh *shawl, Kashmir.*

*Tribal shawl, Bastar.*

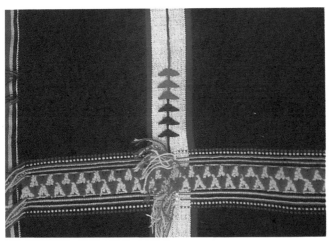

*Tribal shawl, Manipur.*

*Cotton durrie, Uttar Pradesh.*

*The Kashmiri* namdah *(rug).*

# ANCIENT TECHNIQUES

**Phulkari** (cover): *The chief characteristic of phulkari is the horizontal and vertical darn-stitch with which innumerable geometrical patterns are achieved. Soft, untwisted floss silk yarn is embroidered on coarse cloth with a needle about three inches in length. The average size of a phulkari stitch is a quarter of an inch. For a neat finish, the stitches must be even, regular and smooth. This can be confirmed by looking at the reverse side of the fabric where only very small dots should be visible at regular intervals. Sometimes chain-stitch, herring bone-stitch, satin-stitch and stem-stitch are also used. The most prized is the bagh (garden) style wherein the surface of the cloth is so densely embroidered that the embroidery becomes the fabric itself.*

**Ikat** (pages 6 to 11): *The design is predetermined prior to weaving by the manner in which the yarn is tie-dyed. In single-ikat, one of either the warp or weft threads are tie-dyed. In double-ikat, motifs are achieved by a juxtapositioning of similarly dyed shades on equal lengths of warp and weft. Among the double-ikat weaves the most prized is the Patan Patola wherein the warp and the weft synchronize in the weaving with extreme precision to create a rich mosaic. A characteristic feature of ikat is its fuzzy-edged appearance. This is caused by the dye bleeding into tied areas along the yarn.*

**Jamdani** (pages 14 & 15): *Shuttles filled with gold, silver or coloured thread are passed through the warp in accordance with the design. In Uttar Pradesh, white is woven on white, with threads of the same fineness as the fabric. The design is extremely subtle and can be seen clearly only against light. The weavers of Benares have reoriented the* jamdani *into a sort of cut-work. The weft is thrown across the width and after the weaving is complete, the loose threads are cut to create a pattern.*

**Brocade** (pages 25 & 29): *In the usual weaving process the weft thread passes over and under the warp regularly. In the case of brocaded fabrics, special threads are transfixed in between (the intervals depend on the pattern). These threads could be cotton, silk, gold or silver. When gold or silver are used in raised ornamentation, we have* zari-brocade. *When they are used so densely that the ground silk is hardly visible, we have* kinkhab.

**Chikan embroidery** (page 32): *The stitch used is the only ornamentation on the fabric. The effect of* chikan *embroidery is most apparent on fine muslin cloth where the white stitches have a lace-like effect. The design is first block-printed and then embroidered in a variety of ways:* taipchi *is the simple darn-stitch done on muslin;* khatwa *is a combination of fine applique and* taipchi *done on calico;* bakhia *employs the short,* *inverted satin-stitch on fine muslin. The thread is densely massed on the reverse side of the fabric to create a shadowy effect;* jali *is done on netting created by manipulating the warp and the weft of the fabric with the needle;* murri *and* phanda *use the minute satin-stitch in extremely fine knots on muslin.*

**Bandhni** (pages 45 & 46): *Designs are formed by a combination of tiny dots. The pattern is first block-printed on the fabric (veteran craftsmen still make them by free hand). Each dot of the pattern is then tied tightly, using one continuous thread for all. This is done with the aid of a specially cultivated finger nail or a thimble. On elaborate saris the dots can add up to over a hundred thousand knots. After this the fabric is dyed. The tied areas resist the dye and retain their original colour. Earlier vegetable dyes were used though today they are almost always synthetic. The final stage is the removal of the threads though* bandhni *is frequently sold in its tied-up state so that the customer can be sure that it is not a printed imitation.*

**Block-printing** (pages 48 & 49): *The crucial aspect of block-printing is the degree of pressure put on the block to register the design on the fabric. Chemical or vegetable dyes are used. The dye is first poured into a trough. Jute or similar cloth is soaked in the dye with a wire mesh placed over it. Thus the amount of dye released on the block remains controlled. There* are various methods of block-printing. In resist printing, the design is drawn by wax or clay mixed with resin. When the cloth is dyed, these parts retain their original colour. The wax or clay is then washed off with hot water and block-printing is done on the exposed areas. Other methods are discharge printing and alizarine printing.

**Shahtoosh** (page 55): *Among Indian wools, the most prized is the* pashmina, *derived from the Himalayan* pashmina *goat. Selectively sorted for various uses, the finest is referred to as* shahtoosh, *from which is made the famous shahtoosh shawl. The yarn is first soaked in a rice-based solution for added strength after which it is laid out on the loom. While one shuttle turns the weft thread, an extra shuttle is used for the pile threads which are lifted out with a bamboo needle after every five warp threads. Once the weaving is complete, the shawl is washed in* reetha *(soap-nut). The threads are then settled and brushed with the needle. For the final touch, the shawl is rubbed with a black mountain stone. The* shahtoosh *shawl is often referred to as the 'ring shawl' because though it is amazingly warm, it is so soft and light that it can be drawn through a ring.*

*Photo Credits*

*Rupinder Khullar: 13, 45, 49, 54, 55, 59*
*K J Chugh/Fotomedia: 19*
*Ashish Khokar/Fotomedia: 25, 31, 42*
*Marie D'Souza/Fotomedia: 22*
*Amar Talwar/Fotomedia: 48*
*Shalini Saran/Fotomedia: 52*